Fiduciary Mortgage Lending

Matthew Gallagher

Table of Contents

Foreword

With nearly 20 years serving as a financial advisor, I have helped dozens of clients over the years get mortgages on primary or vacation houses and have worked with many mortgage professionals. Many of the mortgage professionals ended up just being salespeople who overpromised and underdelivered by getting a commitment from my clients and then passed the client off to a backoffice team while going in search of the next sale. Generally, the backoffice team would drop the ball on the underwriting, request the same documents two or three times, fail to promptly follow up on questions or requests from the client, and, occasionally, would force the client to have to postpone closing for one reason or another.

After becoming frustrated with many local mortgage brokers due to client complaints or bad customer service experiences, which reflected poorly on me, I was referred to Matt Gallagher. After talking with Matt and understanding his fiduciary philosophy, I decided that, even though he worked in another state, I would give him a try. The results, so far, have been phenomenal. Contrary to my other experiences, Matt and his team have continually underpromised and overdelivered, walked the client through difficult situations, and put the clients interests ahead of their own. I have received many client compliments on how easy and simple Matt and his team made the process, which has only strengthened my relationships with those clients.

Many advisors see mortgage professionals as a commodity and will shop among different mortgage brokers for the cheapest rate, hoping to save the client an eighth of a percent here and there. I once did that as well but then realized that my client's time was valuable and that hidden fees and costs, usually discovered at closing, largely offset that eighth of a percent. While I still will periodically competitively shop rates to keep Matt honest (and he has consistently been lower than or at the competitor's rates), I have directly nearly 100% of my client's mortgages to Matt and his team since we started working together about 5 years ago.

I am proud to have Matt and his team as a resource, knowing that he will be upfront and honest with me and knows that our continued relationship is more important than a quick sale. Ultimately, Matt's focus on transparency, putting the client's interests ahead of his own, and his impeccable focus on customer service and follow through have allowed Matt and his team to earn my trust and the trust of my clients.

Regards,
Aaron Andreas
Arbor Wealth Advisors, LLC
101 W. Big Beaver Road, Suite 1400
Troy, MI 48084

Preface

Everyone tends to overvalue the merits of their profession in their mind. For example, my dentist insists I floss religiously and see him every six months. I don't do either. My mechanic believes I should be very aware of my car's tire pressure, wear, tear, the oil level, age, etc. I'm not. Following this thread, I think the details of your mortgage are more important to you than you likely think they are. I get it. Nevertheless, I rolled up my sleeves and wrote this book as a result of my deep desire to set straight the pervasive misunderstandings about my industry. I work primarily with wealth advisors and/or Certified Public Accountants (CPAs) to help So, allow me to make a handful of points that will help you help your clients.

Fiduciary Conduct

I believe, like a fee-only based wealth manager, mortgage professionals should conduct themselves as fiduciaries.

Quantitative Analysis: I want to show

1. All mortgage questions (except "What are interest rates going to do?") can be answered relatively easily and quantitatively.

2. How I compare two loan offers.

3. How I determine if a loan should be refinanced.

4. How I determine if two loan (or more) should be combined and refinanced.

In today's mortgage industry, Direct Lenders offer clearly better solutions than Correspondent Lenders & Mortgage Brokers. Why?

1. They offer lower non-conforming (a.k.a. "Jumbo") rates.

2. Their Jumbo rates are lower than their conforming rates.

3. They accept higher debt-to-income (DTI) ratios.

4. They allow exceptions.

5. Given 1-4 above, Direct Lenders have a clear competitive advantage over Correspondent Lenders and Mortgage Brokers.

Please understand, in this document, what I am attempting to convey is in general terms and is *my opinion only*. I am discussing what is typical. Meaning, what is likely accurate nine times out of 10. I readily admit, there will be the occasional exception, but what I am teaching is true and accurate the great majority of the time. Also, my comments are focused on the conventional non-conforming / Jumbo loan market. That is my specialty.

Next, I hate the concept of selling. I hate the activity of selling. I truly do. I am fine with business development. That is, of course, necessary. I simply do not believe a person should misrepresent their solution as better than another solution, if it is not. That I consider wrong. Call me naïve, but I believe there is a naturel equilibrium in every market. Fulfill the appropriate level of demand and there is no need to sell. You simply consult & educate.

My industry is one of the worst when it comes to conduct. The promotion of mortgage financing and refinancing is ubiquitous—whether the borrower needs it or not. Advertisements flood the radio, the T.V., direct mail and your Internet browser. Through my experience, I estimate 50% of the refinance transactions that occur, do not benefit the borrower in they way they believe it will.

In my experience, almost all mortgage decisions can be quite easily quantitatively made. The problem is the client doesn't know how to do the math correctly. Often the mortgage loan officer doesn't understand the correct math either, but that doesn't matter as they are motivated to convince and sell—whether the client benefits or not. This behavior should be illegal.

Add to this how long it takes for the conventional wisdom to change. I have been beating the drum for the past seven to eight years trying to get the word out that Jumbo rates are lower than conforming rates at the Direct Lenders. Therefore, there is no need ever to split a loan into two to keep the primary mortgage at the conforming loan level. Yet, after all this time, I still encounter the negative aftermath of this loan structure. If your mortgage loan officer suggests splitting your loan into a conforming first mortgage and a home equity second mortgage this is a red flag, and you are getting subpar advice.

Next, I am asked, "Are you a Broker or do you just represent one bank?" This question stems from the belief a Broker can get you better terms. **This is not true**. Correspondent Lenders & Mortgage Brokers can shop "a market" for rates and chose the best rate from that market for you, but there are multiple mortgage rate markets in the industry, and the market available to the Correspondent Lenders & Mortgage Brokers has higher rates than what you can secure from a Direct Lender. So, if you hear your mortgage loan officer mention they can shop the market, this too is a red flag.

I also hear, "Rates are pretty much the same everywhere." This is unequivocally not true. Needless to say, this too, is a big red flag. If you hear that, I suggest you contact a Direct Lender.

If you stick with me and peruse this document, you will grow to see me as an extension of your team and learn to always call me first when your client has a mortgage situation. I may not always be able to offer the mathematically best terms on the specific transaction, but I am very sure I will provide an unbiased, quantitative answer to the situation. One without the cloud of sales spin. You will also learn how to quantitatively compare two loans, how to accurately assess if your client should refinance their mortgage, how to accurately assess if your client should combine two loans (or more) and refinance them, and that I like to doodle.

I started in the mortgage industry in May of 2005. I am in my 14th year. I have worked for two of the country's largest direct lenders and briefly for a Correspondent Lender. In the entire time I have conducted myself as a fiduciary for my referral sources and their clients. I do not sell. I consult. I quantitatively backup my position. I always do what is right for the client. Like a doctor, I believe, first do no harm. If I cannot unequivocally prove to myself, the referral partner and the client there is a clear benefit, my advice is always to do nothing.

Okay, let's go learn some stuff.

Chapter 1. Introduction

1.1. Fiduciary Conduct

I believe in fiduciary conduct. I believe you should only do what is in the best interest of your client. Mortgage lending is necessary. Mortgage sales is not. Also, as you read this book, and review the exhibits you will see the lengths to which I go to do what is 100% in the best interest of the client. I wish my industry had a fiduciary designation. It should. Regardless, I hold myself to a fiduciary standard.

1.2. Why Direct Lenders Are (presently) Better Than Correspondent Lenders & Mortgage Brokers

They Offer Lower Non-Conforming (a.k.a. "Jumbo") Rates

I routinely see Correspondent Lender and Mortgage Broker rates from .375% to .5%+ higher than the Direct Lender market.

Their Jumbo Rates are Lower than their Conforming Rates

Historically Jumbo loan rates were higher than conforming loan rates. This changed about seven to eight years ago. This means if you need a Jumbo loan amount, this is good, and you will get a lower rate from a Direct Lender. However, if you are working with a Correspondent Lender or Mortgage Broker, since they do not have this beneficial situation, they will encourage you to split your loan into a conforming loan of $X plus a second mortgage of $Y to reach your desired loan amount. This is not a beneficial structure for the client.

They Allow Higher Debt-to-Income (DTI) Ratios

As noted in my preface I am discussing primarily Jumbo mortgages. If a borrower's DTI is > 43% the loan is designated as "non-qualified" or Non-QM for short. A bank must set aside more reserves for Non-QM loans. Direct Lenders will make Non-QM loans to their Retail customers, but they will not buy them from Correspondent Lenders (via the Correspondent Channel), nor from Mortgage Brokers (via the Wholesale Channel). This simply means Correspondent Lenders & Mortgage Brokers maximum DTI is 43% while Direct Lenders can exceed that. In my experience they will typically go up to 50%. Even higher with strong compensating factors. They Allow Exceptions: Every Direct Lender and other Investor in the Jumbo mortgage market has their underwriting rules. An exception simply means you are bending or breaking the Investor's rule. Since Direct Lenders are lending their own money, they can bend rules as they see fit for the Retail Channel, but they will not grant exceptions to the Correspondent or Wholesale Channels.

They Allow Exceptions

Every Direct Lender and other Investor in the Jumbo mortgage market has their underwriting rules. An exception simply means you are bending or breaking the Investor's rule. Since Direct Lenders are lending their own money, they can bend rules as they see fit for the Retail Channel, but they will not grant exceptions to the Correspondent or Wholesale Channels.

1.3. Easy Quantitative Analysis

In every mortgage transaction the numbers are known. I will show you in Chapter 4 how I can make the correct client decision quantitatively. Hence, there is no need for a sales pitch. If you do it my way you can cut through the sales game quickly and come to the correct solution.

1.4. Conclusion

I conduct myself as a fiduciary. I work for a Direct Lender so I can provide higher DTI Ratios & exceptions for qualified borrowers, and I can quantitatively show you how to make decisions. So, there's no need to listen to a sales pitch anymore or to suffer the mortgage nutshell game. Let me show you how to make decisions, quickly, easily and correctly.

Chapter 2. The Mortgage Industry & Its Structure

2.1. The Industry Is Not Efficient

Unlike the stock market where there is one buy price and one sell price for a stock at a particular time, there are thousands of markets for one's mortgage. Efficiency comes from a single market (the NYSE or the NASDAQ, etc.) and from transparency. The mortgage industry has neither. There is not one market. There are thousands of markets. Each investor for a mortgage (a Direct Lender, a Hedge Fund, Fannie Mae, Freddie Mac, etc.) has its own pricing variables for a loan. For example, at the Direct Lender for whom I work, I counted 87 variables that affect the final rate on our portfolio 30YF Jumbo loan. We have 58 loan products available. Not all loan products have 87 variables that affect the final rate, but for fun let's just say they do. That is 58 loan products times 87 pricing variables = 5,046 total variables. And that is just one Direct Lender. Add to this equation Chase, Bank of America, Wells Fargo, Citi Mortgage, US Bank, SunTrust, BB&T, Associated Bank, etc. and you are quickly into the many tens of thousands of variables, potentially you would even be over 100,000 variables. As for transparency you would have to contact a representative from every lender, about 20 to 30 total, make sure your variables are exactly the same, get a Loan Estimate from each, and then do an apples-to-apples comparison. That's asking a lot. Someday, I think there will be a mortgage exchange. Many firms are working on this. If, and when that happens, you will see the margins in the industry get squashed. Just like what happened to the NASDAQ market makers when the ECN (Electronic Communication Network) was introduced. Spreads went from $.25 - $.375 per share to $.05, and

I believe now they are at about $.01 per share.

What do You Mean There is Not a Single Market?

That's right. There are many thousands of markets. Each lender creates their own market. They borrow or buy money at one rate, mark it up as they see fit and resell or lend it at a higher rate. Just like in any industry there are myriad factors that affect the end price. For example, there are economies of scale. The larger the lender, the more likely they can borrow their money at lower cost. For example, the big banks with billions in deposits are borrowing that money at very likely less than 1%. So, call that their cost of funds. Other lenders—the Correspondent Lenders—have to borrow money from a larger bank and use it to fund their loans. They are paying short term loan rates for their funds—not deposit rates, so their money costs them more. Then the lender has to determine how much to mark up their costs. The mark up will be a function of the market, the lender's brand, etc. For example, one lender may offer their loans at a lower rate to attract new business. Another will try to price in the middle of the market and rely on their brand name to attract business. Other lenders may try to charge a premium. Typically, this only works if they have a very strong brand name, an extremely loyal or ignorant client base. *So, add the many tens of thousands to over 100,000 variables in the market times the number of mortgage companies out there utilizing different pricing structures and you have a highly inefficient market.*

2.2. Types of Mortgage Loans

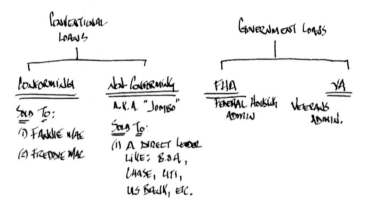

Conventional Loans

Conventional mortgage loans are not insured by a government agency like the Federal Housing Administration (FHA) or the Veterans Administration (VA). Conventional loans are funded by Fannie Mae (Fannie), Freddie Mac (Freddie) or a Direct Lender.

Conventional Conforming

Conventional conforming loans are loans that qualify to be purchased by Fannie or Freddie. Fannie & Freddie guarantee the timely payment of principal & interest on the loans they purchase. Given this guarantee, they can borrow at lower rates, which are passed on to borrowers. While there are hundreds of criteria for a loan to meet Fannie or Freddie guidelines, the most well-known criteria is the loan amount. As of January 1, 2019, the loan amount is $484,300. Anything less than or equal to this amount is eligible on that criteria. Any loan greater than $484,300 is considered Jumbo, or non-conforming. With that said, in certain high value counties the Fannie / Freddie loan limit is higher. You must check county-by-county.

Conventional Non-conforming / Jumbo

As noted above, there are hundreds of criteria that make a loan non-conforming, but the most common is the loan amount, which is presently $484,300. If a loan does not meet all of Fannie or Freddie's criteria it is non-conforming (it does not conform to their guidelines). Who provides the funding for these loans? Direct Lenders. Direct Lenders are the large, nationwide banks, super regional banks and non-traditional lenders. A partial list of Direct Lenders is Chase, Bank of America, Wells Fargo, Citi Mortgage, US Bank, SunTrust, BB&T, Associated Bank, etc.

Government Loans

FHA

FHA stands for Federal Housing Administration. FHA loans are insured by the FHA. FHA loans were created to provide mortgage funding for lower credit quality borrowers than Fannie or Freddie. FHA loans allow for lower credit scores and lower down payments (as low as 3.5%). FHA loans carry lower interest rates, but substantially higher fees. Apples-to-apples, per my **Loan Comparison Worksheet** , you need to stay in an FHA loan for five years for the lower monthly payment to offset the higher upfront costs.

VA

VA stands for Veterans Administration. VA loans are insured by the VA. They were created to provide mortgage financing for veterans and their surviving spouses. VA loans also allow lower credit scores and lower down payments (as low as 0%). VA loans carry lower rates, and often higher fees. The fees situation is a bit complicated as certain fees are waived for disabled veterans. To calculation which is better, VA or conforming, simply follow the steps outlined in Chapter IV, Easy Quantitative Analysis, Section B, How to Compare Two Loans. Or, email me and I'll do it for you.

Non-Traditional

This segment of the market is growing rapidly from a percentage perspective yet remains quite small from a total dollar standard. In time though, expect this segment to innovate, disrupt and capture a larger share of the market. This is where I expect a mortgage exchange to come from and is also where Correspondent Lenders and Mortgage Brokers could become competitive again.

2.3. The Three Types of Mortgage Lenders

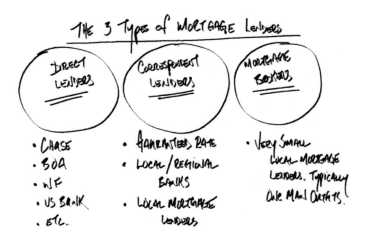

THE 3 Types of MORTGAGE Lenders

DIRECT LENDERS
- CHASE
- BOA
- WF
- US BANK
- ETC.

CORRESPONDENT LENDERS
- GUARANTEED RATE
- LOCAL/REGIONAL BANKS
- LOCAL MORTGAGE LENDERS

MORTGAGE BROKERS
- Very Small Local Mortgage Lenders. Typically One Man Outfits.

Type 1: Direct Lenders

As noted above, Direct Lenders are the large, nationwide or super regional banks and non-traditional lenders like hedge funds. A partial list of Direct Lenders is Chase, Bank of America, Wells Fargo, Citi Mortgage, US Bank, SunTrust, BB&T, etc. **Here's the big secret. Direct Lenders have two or three channels through which they do mortgage business.** This is very important to understand.

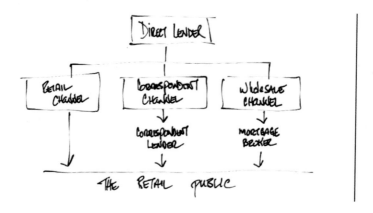

The Retail Channel

The retail channel lends directly to borrowers via bank locations, mortgage offices or the Internet. Direct Lenders offer lower Jumbo rates, higher DTI ratios and exceptions through their Retail Channel. For example, I work in the Retail Channel of a Direct Lender in St. Louis, MO.

The Correspondent Channel

This channel purchases loans from Correspondent Lenders. Direct Lenders offer higher Jumbo rates, lower DTI ratios and allow no exceptions through their Correspondent Channels. *In the past they did, but this changed about seven to eight years ago.*

The Wholesale Channel

Direct Lenders make loans to borrowers via a Mortgage Brokers through their Wholesale Channels. Many Direct Lenders have shut down their Wholesale Channels.

Pros of Direct Lenders

1. *Lower Jumbo Rates*

As noted, Direct Lenders lend money to borrowers through their Retail Channel, their Correspondent Channel and their Wholesale Channel (if applicable). Why are rates lower to the consumer through the Retail Channel.

After the Financial Crisis Direct Lenders Made the Business Decision to Offer Lower Jumbo Rate via the Retail Channel: After the housing crisis it took longer for the commercial side of the economy to start borrowing than the Direct Lenders anticipated. They found themselves with very large supplies of cash to lend, but very little commercial demand. Hence, they made the decision to lend this excess supply of cash through their Retail Channels to Jumbo mortgage borrowers. I remember when this happened. Every day I check interest rates, and our Jumbo rates were about .5% or more less than the day before. I called our Capital Markets Group to see what was going on they explained the situation. This occurred roughly seven to eight years ago. ***Centers of influence and borrowers still have not caught on.***

2. ***Jumbo Rates are Lower than the Conforming loan rates***

Following closely on the point above, at the Direct Lenders Jumbo loan rates fell significantly below conforming loan rates. Again, it has been this way for seven to eight years, yet I still encounter surprise from borrowers when I explain this to them. "Really? Jumbo rates are lower than conforming rates?" "YES!" This also raises a very important point. Very often if a borrower needs to borrow an amount higher than the conforming loan limit, since they wrongly think Jumbo rates are higher, they will split the amount they need to borrow into a 1st mortgage at the conforming limit, say $484,300, and then take out a 2nd mortgage (a.k.a. home equity loan) to make up the difference. ***This is typically NOT the optimal debt structure for the client.*** For example, using real world rates from January 31, 2019, assume someone is purchasing a $700,000 house and they have 20% to put down.

a. Using a Conforming loan

    i. Purchase price = $700,000

    ii. -Down payment = $140,000 (20%)

    iii. =Required loan amount = $560,000 (80%)

    iv. If the mortgage loan officer doesn't work for a Direct Lender, his/her conforming loan rates will be lower than their Jumbo loan rates. Hence, they will likely split the loan as follows:

        A. 1st mortgage = $484,300 (maximum conforming limit) @ ~4.5%

        B. +2nd mortgage = $75,700 @ ~6%

        C. =$560,000 @ a weighted average rate of ~4.703%.

b. Using a Jumbo Loan

    i. Purchase price = $700,000

    ii. -Down payment = $140,000 (20%)

    iii. =Required loan amount = $560,000 (80%) @ ~4.125%.

The Jumbo Loan structure is better for the client in two ways. First, 4.125% is clearly better than the weighted average rate of 4.703%. Second, 2nd mortgages are typically floating rate loans. Yes, you can set them as fixed rate loans, but most of the time clients take the interest-only, floating rate option. Hence, using this structure, the client is exposed to interest rate risk. The one Jumbo loan solution removes interest rate risk.

3. *Higher DTI Ratios*

Since a Direct Lender is lending their own money, they have more flexibility. For example, via a Correspondent Lender, on a Jumbo loan the maximum DTI is 43%. However, in the Direct Lender world, it's easy to lend to 50% DTI, and I have seen them go higher. Why is this? A loan with a DTI ratio higher than 43% is considered a non-qualified mortgage (Non-QM) under the Dodd Frank Financial Reform Act. Non-QM loans require a bank to hold more reserves. Direct Lenders will not purchase Non-QM loans from Correspondent Lenders and Mortgage Brokers. ***Hence, greater than 43% DTI is not available outside the Direct Lender Retail Channel.*** Seven percent DTI may not seem significant, but it is. For example, assuming a borrower earns $100,000 a year. At a 43% DTI the borrower can have maximum debt of $43,000, or $3583 per month. At a 50% DTI they can have maximum debt of $50,000, or $4166 per month. That monthly differential of $583 ($4166-$3583) at 4.4375% on a 30YF loan will finance $116,900. For someone making $200,000 per year, they can borrow an additional $233,800. While I most certainly do not encourage people to borrow up to a 50% DTI, it comes in very handy when the borrower wishes to purchase, close and move into their new home, before selling their old home. This is not only far more convenient, it can help a borrower avoid liquidating assets at an inopportune time.

Exceptions

Direct Lenders and other investors have underwriting policies and guidelines. Of course. An exception simply means you are bending or breaking from policy. For example, say a borrower's DTI is higher than policy allows, but they have a very strong asset position. A Direct Lender can make the decision to grant an exception and do the loan. Mortgage Lending guidelines are driven by many regulatory agencies (for example, The Office of the Comptroller of the Currency (OCC), the FDIC, etc.) and many regulations (for example, Dodd-Frank Financial Reform). As above, if the loan doesn't meet the OCC or Dodd-Frank guidelines it is Non-QM and the bank must hold more reserves. Direct Lenders will not purchase Non-QM loans through their Correspondent or Wholesale Channels. *Hence, exceptions are only available through the Direct Lender Retail Channel.*

Cons of Direct Lenders

Each Direct Lender has one set of products. For example, say Direct Lender A has a great program for doctors, but Direct Lender B does not. If I work for Direct Lender B, and you are a doctor, I cannot offer you that program. Another example could be that Direct Lender C has a really good program for individuals with a lot of financial assets, but not a lot of income. Say then have $8,000,000 in savings, but their income is merely $40,000 from Social Security. Clearly the $8,000,000 in assets justifies a home of a value higher than their $40,000 Social Security income. Well, if the borrower walks into a Direct Lender location without this product, they may never hear about it. Correspondent Lenders and Mortgage Brokers have access to the programs of multiple Direct Lenders. Of course, being a fiduciary, I send clients to other banks all the time if they have a product that suits them better than what I have.

Type 2: Correspondent Lenders

First and foremost, everyone outside my industry mistakes Correspondent Lenders for Mortgage Brokers. The terms are used interchangeably, but there is a BIG difference. Correspondent Lenders fund your loan at closing with their own money. As they are using their own funds, they are taking risk, and they earn additional income for said risk. They hold the loan on their balance sheet for a few weeks, and then they sell the loan to Fannie, Freddie, FHA, VA or a Direct Lender (Bank of America, Chase, Citi Mortgage, Wells Fargo, US Bank, SunTrust, BB&T, etc.). There are very few nationwide Correspondent Lenders. Guaranteed Rate is one that comes to mind. Mostly, they are the local mortgage companies where your "guy" or "friend" works. They are the companies you hear aggressively marketing on the radio, the T.V., direct mail or your Internet browser. They are also the small local and regional banks in your area. Very few people know this, but unless you are going to a Direct Lender—even if you are at a bank—you are not getting the best terms available in the market. Some Correspondent Lenders are very good, well run companies. Some are very bad and are merely marketing machines that could as easily be selling windows, gutters or siding, yet mortgages are their widget.

Pros of Correspondent Lenders

Access to multiple Direct Lenders, and therefore, access to multiple programs. For example, while working briefly for a Correspondent Lender one of their sources had a program that allowed a borrower to be approved for a loan as long as they had 180 months of principal, interest, taxes & insurance (PITI), or housing payments. That is a good program, and it might just solve the problem for the people with a lot of assets, but not a lot of income. Of course, unique solutions like this carry higher interest rates. Regardless, it is a good solution, and if I cannot solve a client's issue via my product solutions, I will tell them about this one and refer them over to this Correspondent Lender.

Cons of Correspondent Lenders

1. *Higher Jumbo Loan Rates*

   As covered above, in the Direct Lender section. Direct Lenders have lower Jumbo rates. So, yes, your Correspondent Lender can shop the market for you, but they are shopping a pool of higher rates set up for them by the Direct Lenders.

2. *Jumbo Loan Rates are Higher than Conforming Loan Rates*

   In the Correspondent Lender world, Jumbo rates remain higher then conforming loan rates. This is undoubtedly a disadvantage for the borrower. Plus, they are more likely to end up with split loan scenarios like the example under Direct Lender Pros.

3. *43% Maximum DTI Ratio*

   Direct Lenders will only buy loans from Correspondents that have DTIs less than or equal to 43%. Hence, Correspondent Lenders are capped at 43% DTI

No Exceptions

As discussed in the Direct Lender Pros section. Direct Lenders can make exceptions, but they will not buy loans from Correspondent Lenders with exceptions Hence,

Correspondent Lenders cannot provide exceptions. This is a clear disadvantage.

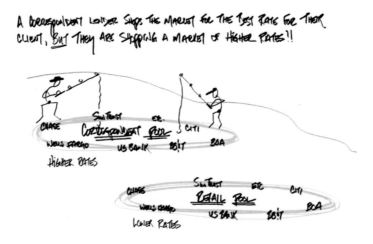

Type 3: Mortgage Brokers

Mortgage Brokers merely bring together a borrower and a Direct Lender. They do not fund the loan and then sell it. They merely complete some paperwork. As they have no risk, they earn no other revenue than that which they can add to the transaction in the form of points or origination fees. Hence, in my experience, Mortgage Brokers always charge substantially higher fees than Direct & Correspondent Lenders.

Pros of Mortgage Brokers

I see no advantage to ever working with a Mortgage Broker. All things being equal, you should always get better terms from a Correspondent Lender. And, if it is a Jumbo loan, you will get even better terms from a Direct Lender.

Cons of Mortgage Brokers

Everything. I see no benefit to ever work with a Mortgage

Broker. You will do better at a Correspondent Lender, and better yet at a Direct Lender.

Chapter 3. The Government's Tools to Help You Compare Loans

3.1. The Annual Percentage Rate (APR)

It is a common misunderstanding that the loan with the lower APR is the lower cost, and better loan for you. Unfortunately, this is not the case. As, with many government outcomes, APR started as a good idea, but once it passed through Congress, the Senate, was signed into law, and implemented by the regulators it was not what was originally intended. You see, the regulators never specifically detailed precisely how to calculate the APR. # 1 So, if you have an equation that can be calculated in more than one way, well, it is meaningless.

3.2. The Loan Estimate

A sample Loan Estimate is below.

FICUS BANK

4321 Random Boulevard · Somecity, ST 12340

Save this Loan Estimate to compare with your Closing Disclosure.

Loan Estimate

DATE ISSUED	2/15/2013
APPLICANTS	Michael Jones and Mary Stone
	123 Anywhere Street
	Anytown, ST 12345
PROPERTY	456 Somewhere Avenue
	Anytown, ST 12345
SALE PRICE	$180,000

LOAN TERM	30 years
PURPOSE	Purchase
PRODUCT	Fixed Rate
LOAN TYPE	☒ Conventional ☐FHA ☐VA ☐_____
LOAN ID #	123456789
RATE LOCK	☐ NO ☒ YES, until 4/16/2013 at 5:00 p.m. EDT

*Before closing, your interest rate, points, and lender credits can change unless you lock the interest rate. All other estimated closing costs expire on **3/4/2013** at 5:00 p.m. EDT*

Loan Terms

		Can this amount increase after closing?
Loan Amount	$162,000	NO
Interest Rate	3.875%	NO
Monthly Principal & Interest *See Projected Payments below for your Estimated Total Monthly Payment*	$761.78	NO

	Does the loan have these features?
Prepayment Penalty	YES · **As high as $3,240** if you pay off the loan during the first 2 years
Balloon Payment	NO

Projected Payments

Payment Calculation	Years 1-7		Years 8-30	
Principal & Interest		$761.78		$761.78
Mortgage Insurance	+	82	+	—
Estimated Escrow *Amount can increase over time*	+	206	+	206
Estimated Total Monthly Payment		**$1,050**		**$968**

		This estimate includes	In escrow?
Estimated Taxes, Insurance & Assessments *Amount can increase over time*	$206 a month	☒ Property Taxes ☒ Homeowner's Insurance ☐ Other:	YES YES

See Section G on page 2 for escrowed property costs. You must pay for other property costs separately.

Costs at Closing

Estimated Closing Costs	$8,054	Includes $5,672 in Loan Costs + $2,382 in Other Costs – $0 in Lender Credits. *See page 2 for details.*
Estimated Cash to Close	$16,054	Includes Closing Costs. *See Calculating Cash to Close on page 2 for details.*

Visit **www.consumerfinance.gov/mortgage-estimate** for general information and tools.

Figure 1. Sample loan estimate (page 1)

Closing Cost Details

Loan Costs	
A. Origination Charges	**$1,802**
.25 % of Loan Amount (Points)	$405
Application Fee	$300
Underwriting Fee	$1,097

Other Costs	
E. Taxes and Other Government Fees	**$85**
Recording Fees and Other Taxes	$85
Transfer Taxes	

F. Prepaids	$867
Homeowner's Insurance Premium (6 months)	$605
Mortgage Insurance Premium (months)	
Prepaid Interest ($17.44 per day for 15 days @ 3.875%)	$262
Property Taxes (months)	

G. Initial Escrow Payment at Closing		$413
Homeowner's Insurance	$100.83 per month for 2 mo.	$202
Mortgage Insurance	per month for mo.	
Property Taxes	$105.30 per month for 2 mo.	$211

B. Services You Cannot Shop For	$672
Appraisal Fee	$405
Credit Report Fee	$30
Flood Determination Fee	$20
Flood Monitoring Fee	$32
Tax Monitoring Fee	$75
Tax Status Research Fee	$110

H. Other	$1,017
Title – Owner's Title Policy (optional)	$1,017

I. TOTAL OTHER COSTS (E + F + G + H)	$2,382

C. Services You Can Shop For	$3,198
Pest Inspection Fee	$135
Survey Fee	$65
Title – Insurance Binder	$700
Title – Lender's Title Policy	$535
Title – Settlement Agent Fee	$502
Title – Title Search	$1,261

J. TOTAL CLOSING COSTS	$8,054
D + I	$8,054
Lender Credits	

Calculating Cash to Close	
Total Closing Costs (J)	$8,054
Closing Costs Financed (Paid from your Loan Amount)	$0
Down Payment/Funds from Borrower	$18,000
Deposit	– $10,000
Funds for Borrower	$0
Seller Credits	$0
Adjustments and Other Credits	$0
Estimated Cash to Close	**$16,054**

D. TOTAL LOAN COSTS (A + B + C)	$5,672

Figure 2. Sample loan estimate (page 2)

The Loan Estimate is a regulated document that must be given to a borrower within three days of applying for a loan. The Loan Estimate details the sale price or appraised value, the loan term, the loan purpose, the product, loan amount, interest rate, principal + interest payment, mortgage insurance payment (if applicable) estimated taxes, estimated insurance, loan costs, prepaid items, lender credits (if applicable) and the amount of cash you will need to bring to closing. Again, as with APR, the objective was to provide borrowers with a tool to help them compare loans. Unfortunately, the end result is a bit of a mess. I actually wrote to HUD suggesting they add a total of Section A & Section B costs which are the variable, lender-related fees, and some of the most important numbers. They sent me a seven-page letter explaining why it was done this way. The problem with the Loan Estimate is some of the numbers on it are variable based on the lender you choose, and some will not vary based on the lender you choose. To make matters worse, all the non-variable numbers are estimated by each lender. So, Lender A may estimate these non-variable numbers at $X, and Lender B may estimate them at $Y, yet in the final analysis they will be $Z. Regardless of the estimates, they will be $Z. This is going to be boring, but I am going to walk you through the Loan Estimate section-by-section. Yay for you! Quick Tangent—this is going to get easier in Chapter IV. There are a lot of numbers on the Loan Estimate. It varies, but on one I counted 66 numbers. As noted above, only a handful of the numbers matter when it comes to comparing two loans. On the same one where I counted 66 numbers, only 12 numbers mattered for the sake of comparison. So, soldier on with me knowing that in Chapter IV, I am going to make this easy for you.

Variable Lender-Related Terms & Fees:

I have highlighted these in light green

Variable Lender-Related Terms

1. Product

2. Loan Amount

3. Interest Rate

4. Mortgage Insurance

Variable Lender-Related Fees

These, too, are highlighted in light green. These can be found on page 2, section A and section B. There is one more variable lender-related item. It is hidden in section J: Lender Credits. It's the opposite of a fee and is an important number as you will see in Chapter IV where I show you how I compare two loans.

Section A: *Origination Charges*

These numbers will vary by lender. So, for the sake of comparing two loans, they are important. You must factor these numbers into your comparison.

Section B: *Services You Cannot Shop For*

These numbers, too, will vary by lender and are important when it comes to comparing two loans. Factor these into your comparison.

Non-Variable Fees & Prepaid Items

These are highlighted in pink. When it comes to comparing two loans, you can throw out every number from here on, except for two caveats, section C, and section J.

Section C: *Services You Can Shop For*

I promised this would be easy in Chapter IV, and it will. This is the only tricky part. On a purchase transaction these fees will be 100% exactly the same regardless of lender. Therefore, you can throw them out of your analysis. However, on a refinance transaction, these fees will vary by lender, but only slightly. So, on a purchase, ignore them. On a refinance, factor them in. However; overall, you can more or less always ignore them as I will show you in Chapter IV and it's easy. With that said, let me explain, why on a purchase transaction—while each lender will estimate these numbers differently—they will all be precisely the same at closing.

Pest Inspection Fee

Your Realtor will refer you to a company that does this, or you will pick your own. Regardless, while the lender tosses in a number, the actual, final number will be whatever you spent. You will tell the title company, and they will tell the lender, and the lender will plug it in. So, Lender A may estimate $200. Lender B may estimate $300. The final number will be whatever it is you spent.

Survey

Exactly the same. Your Realtor or the title company will recommend a firm. You'll pick a firm and spend $X. Hence, it really doesn't matter what the lender estimated it to be. It is what it is. So, when comparing, you'll get a better outcome if you throw out such non-variables.

Title-Insurance Binder

Same.

Title-Lender's Title Policy

Same.

Title-Settlement Agent Fee

Same.

Title-Title Search

Same.

Section E: *Taxes & Other Government Fees*

Recording Fees & Other Taxes

The County in which your property is located will charge $X per page to record the mortgage or deed of trust. Most mortgages and deeds of trust are the same number of pages or within a page or two of each other. So, while this number could vary $1 or $2 per lender, I'm calling it a non-variable fee. Throw it out.

Transfer Taxes

These too will be dictated by the County or State government. They will not vary by lender. They are what they are.

Section F: *Prepaids*

Homeowner's Insurance Premium

Your property must be insured effective the day of closing. You will shop for and purchase this policy. You will pay for it prior to, or at closing. Regardless, again, while a lender will estimate this number, you will give the title company the information and they will give it to your lender. This number will not vary by lender.

Prepaid Interest

This is the interest on your new loan from the day of closing to the end of the month. You will close on the same day regardless of lender. So, in the final analysis, this number will be the same no matter which lender you choose. But, on the Loan Estimate, one lender may assume you close on the first or the month, and another may assume you close on the 30th of the month. Therefore, on the estimate this number can be different by thousands of dollars. Yet, in the end, it will be what it will be. For the sake of comparing two loan throw this number out.

Section G: *Initial Escrow Payment at Closing*

Homeowner's Insurance

First, I am getting pretty bored explaining all of this. I can only imagine how bored you are if you are still reading. If so, good for you. All you are doing here is taking the cost of about two or three months of your homeowner's insurance and moving it from one of your savings accounts to an escrow account at the bank. Again, it is what it is. It's not variable. Throw it out of your analysis.

Property Taxes

Precisely the same as the homeowner's insurance. It is what it is. Toss it out of your analysis.

Section H: *Other*

Title-Owner's Policy (Optional)

Just more title insurance costs. Each lender will estimate the number, but it will be what it will be. It's not a variable. Remove it from your analysis.

3.3. What are Closing Costs?

There is a big difference between closing costs and estimate cash to close, and this confuses the heck out of consumers. There is no definition of closing costs, so I consider closing costs, any actual cost related to the mortgage transaction. I do not consider closing costs to be the costs and fees that you would have encountered regardless. This means they are merely the costs of homeownership or interest on a loan.

Actual Closing Costs

I consider actual closing costs to be lender related fees, inspection fees, title fees government fees.

Estimated Cash to Close

Estimated cash to close is actual closing costs plus prepaid items (homeowner's insurance, and the establishment of escrow accounts).

Chapter 4. Easy Quantitative Analysis

4.1. The Misguided Focus on Rate

Repeat after me, *"Term is more important than rate. Term is more important than rate. Term is more important than rate."* Okay, let's learn some very helpful stuff.

When contemplating mortgage financing the first question always is, "What is the rate?" Yet, when it comes to saving money, the most important aspect of your loan is the term—the number of months over which you will repay your loan. I always knew most of one's savings came from term, but I had never done the math. So, I used this real-world scenario below, and crunched the numbers to find out. Let's just say I was SHOCKED by what I learned. It was November 1, 2018 and I was just given the following transaction with which to assist.

- Purchase
- Second home
- Single family
- Salt Lake City, UT
- Purchase price = $517,500
- --Down payment = $103,500 (20%)
- =Loan amount = $414,000 (80%)

My rates for this transaction that day were:

1. 30YF = 4.875%

2. 20YF = 4.75%

3. 15YF = 4.375%

4. 10YF = 4.125%

Using the above referenced transaction and rates, below is a table showing four financing scenarios: the product, the rate, the monthly payment, the # of payments, and the total, life of loan payments.

Product	Rate	P+i Payment	Number of Payments	Life of Loan Payments
30YF	4.875%	$2,191	360	$788,732
20YF	4.75%	$2,675	240	$642,088
15YF	4.375%	$3,141	180	$565,324
10YF	4.125%	$4,216	120	$505,942

The savings between the 30YF loan and the 20YF loan

Product	Rate	P+i Payment	Number of Payments	Life of Loan Payments
30YF	4.875%	$2,191	360	$788,732
20YF	4.75%	$2,675	240	$642,088
			Savings	**$146,644**

So, by utilizing a 20YF loan compared to a 30YF loan, you will save $146,644. How much of that is due to the lower rate and how much is due to the shorter term? To do this, isolate the term savings by setting the 20YF loan rate equal to the 30YF loan rate of 4.875%. By so doing, all the savings we find will be based on the shorter term alone. This math is below.

Product	Rate	P+i Payment	Number of Payments	Life of Loan Payments
30YF	4.875%	$2,191	360	$788,732
20YF	**4.875%**	$2,704	240	$648,890
			Savings due to Term	**$139,842 (95%)**
			Savings due to Rate	**$6,803 (5%)**

Are you shocked by this math? I was. Of the $146,644 savings, $139,842, or 95% of the savings is due to the term! This means only $6,803, or 5% of the savings is due to the interest rate. The term is 20 times more important than the rate! I found this so surprising I did the math comparing the 30YF to the 15YF. See below.

The savings between the 30YF loan and the 15YF loan

Product	Rate	P+i Payment	Number of Payments	Life of Loan Payments
30YF	4.875%	$2,191	360	$788,732
15YF	4.375%	$3,141	180	$565,324
			Savings	**$233,408**

So, by utilizing a 15YF loan compared to a 30YF loan, you will save $233,408. How much of that is due to the lower rate and how much is due to the shorter term? Here we go again. To do this, isolate the term savings by setting the 15YF loan rate equal to the 30YF loan rate of 4.875%. By so doing, all the savings we find will be based on the shorter term alone.

Product	Rate	P+i Payment	Number of Payments	Life of Loan Payments
30YF	4.875%	$2,191	360	$788,732
15YF	**4.875%**	$3,247	180	$584,458
		Savings due to Term		**$204,273 (91%)**
		Savings due to Rate		**$19,135 (9%)**

Of the $233,408 in savings you would achieve by financing your loan on a 15YF compared to a 30YF, 91% of the savings ($204,274 / $233,408) is due to the term. Only 9%, or $19,315 are due to the interest rate. In this case the term is 11 times more important than the rate. Again, I was so surprised by this math I had to go the next step and look into the savings between the 30YF and the 10YF.

The savings between the 30YF loan and the 10YF loan

Product	Rate	P+i Payment	Number of Payments	Life of Loan Payments
30YF	4.875%	$2,191	360	$788,732
10YF	4.125%	$4,216	120	$523,903
			Savings	**$282,790**

You would save $282,790 if you utilized a 10YF rather than a 30YF on this loan. Again, let's see how much of this is due to the term, and how much is due to the rate. Isolate the term savings by setting the 10YF rate equal to the 30YF rate of 4.875%. The results are below.

Product	Rate	P+i Payment	Number of Payments	Life of Loan Payments
30YF	4.875%	$2,191	360	$788,732
10YF	**4.875%**	$4,365	120	$523,903
		Savings due to Term		**$264,829 (94%)**
		Savings due to Rate		**$17,961 (6%)**

Here we go again. Of the original $282,790 in savings, $264,829, or 94% is due to the term. Only $17,961, or 6% is due to the rate. Again, we lean the term is 15 times more important that the rate.

What I want you to learn from the foregoing exercise is that TERM is far more important than RATE when it comes to saving money on your loan. Of course, all things be equal, yes, rate is important. But rarely are all things equal. Knowing how important term will is be helpful as you read the rest of this most important chapter.

4.2. How to Compare Two Loans

First, the government has not made it easy to compare loans. They created the APR and the Loan Estimate. Both have their problems as outlined in Chapter III. Since you cannot rely on APR and cannot simply look at the Estimated Cash to Close number on the loan Estimate, how do you compare two loan offers? Remember from Chapter III there are variable lender related fees, and there are a bunch of non-variable, non-lender related fees. *I compare only the variable lender related terms and fees. I ignore all non-variable, non-lender-related costs and fees.* This will make more sense after seeing my solution. First you should get a written estimate with detailed line-by-line costs. If the loan officer with who you are working will not provide this, move on to another loan officer. That's ridiculous. If they want to send an email saying "closing costs" will be about $X,XXX, move on. Remember from Chapter III, what are closing costs? Does the $X,XXX number include the variable closing costs, or all the closing costs, or the closing costs plus the prepaid items. If the loan officer will not provide a detailed, line-by-line, cost estimate I would find another loan officer. Why am I spending so much time slicing and dicing the different types of costs? *Because there is an inverse relationship between costs and rates!* As variable lender-related costs increase, the rate can go down. That should make intuitive sense. So, of course, on the other hand, as variable lender-related costs go down, the rate goes up. An unscrupulous loan officer will toy with fees to make their rate look better.

The Loan Comparison Worksheet

A real world sample Loan Comparison Worksheet is below.

Using this example, let's go step-by-step through how I compare two loan offers.

1. *Line up the different lender's terms quoted to make sure you are comparing apples-to-apples.* By lender terms I mean:

   a. *The same purchase price:* In this case the purchase price for both lenders is $625,000. So, "check".

   b. *The same loan amount:* Both lenders are quoting based on a loan of $448,000. Check.

   c. *The same loan product:* Both lenders are quoting a 15YF loan. Check.

2. *Calculate the positives and negatives between the different terms.* In short, calculate the difference in the monthly principal and interest payments. If there is mortgage insurance, add that in. Mortgage insurance will vary by lender. So, now you have half of the information you need: which lender, if either is offering you the lowest monthly payment and by how much. In this example Bank 1's rate is 3.95%. Bank 2's rate is 3.99%. Bank 1's rate is .04% better, and this equates to $9 month.

3. *Calculate each lender's total variable, lender related fees.* Remember, these are the all of the fees on page 2, sections A & B of the Loan Estimate minus any lender credits from section J. After you have done this, you now know what each lender is charging you for the interest rate they are quoting. Calculate the difference in costs between the lenders. In this example Bank 1's total variable lender related fees are $1,199. Bank 2's total lender related fees are a negative $130. Meaning after the lender credits they are giving the borrower, there will still be $130 left that the borrower can apply to other fees. So, the difference in costs between these to offers is $1,329 ($1,199 + $130).

4. *Calculate a breakeven.* In this case, Bank 1 offers a lower rate which equates to $9 per month in savings. However, Bank 1's fees are $1,329 higher than Bank 2's fees. The breakeven is $1,329 / $9 = 148 months. This means it will take 148 months for the $9 per month savings to add up to the $1,329 in savings. You can see in my notes, I think 148 months to breakeven is way too far in the future, but, as always, I defer to the wealth advisor / CPA and the client. This is very simple, and after almost 14 years in the business, I have not discovered a better way to do it.

Loan Terms:

Lender:		Bank 1		Bank 2		Diff
Loan amount:		$ 448,000		$ 448,000		
Down payment/equity:		$ 177,000		$ 177,000		
Purchase price/appraised value:		$ 625,000		$ 625,000	$	-
Product:		15YF		15YF		
Term in months:		180		180		
Rate:		3.950%		3.990%		-0.040%
Payment:	$	3,303	$	3,312	$	(9)
PMI:	$	-	$	-	$	-
Total loan payment:	**$**	**3,303**	**$**	**3,312**	**$**	**(9)**

Variable costs: (Loan Estimate Sections A & B):

Bank 1 Fees:

Closing:	$	100		
Processing:	$	395		
Appraisal:	$	500		
Credit report:	$	28		
Electronic document delivery:	$	12		
Flood certification:	$	10		
Tax service:	$	85		
Verification of tax return:	$	69		

Bank 2 Fees:

Application:			$	395
Commitment:			$	375
Appraisal:			$	400
Tax service:			$	80
Credit report:			$	32
Flood:			$	8
Lender credit based on interest rate:	$	-	$	(1,120)
Bank 2 credit for opening a _____ Checking:	$	-	$	(300)
Total variable costs:	**$**	**1,199**	**$**	**(130)**	**$**	**1,329**

███████

Here's how I look at two loans. First, compare the terms. Bank 1 is if offering the better rate: 3.95% vs. 3.99%. This equates to a savings of $9 per month.

Next, compare the variable, lender-related fees. Bank 1's fees are $1199. Our fees are actually a negative $129. Hence, we are $1329 lower in fees.

Breakeven: $1329 in higher costs for / $9 per month in a lower rate = 148 months or 12 years. Meaning, it will take 12 years for their $9/month savings to add up to the lower costs we charged them. To me, 12 years is far too long a breakeven, but I defer to you.

Any questions, call me.

Matt Gallagher

███████

4.3. Should You Refinance? *The Refinance Analysis*

This is where it all began for me. When I entered the industry in 2005 there were still a lot of people who could benefit from refinancing their loan. I quickly realized people often thought they were saving money simply because their loan payment went down. People did not understand how much of their payment reduction was merely because they increased their loan term and how much was due to the lower interest rate. Therefore, I created the *Refinance Analysis.* This document shows a client and their wealth advisor / CPA quickly and easily the precise data one needs to know when considering refinancing: their payment change, their true savings change (if any), their precise costs and their breakeven. As we learned, the loan term is the most important number when it comes to saving money on your loan, and it is the variable most often manipulated or simply misunderstood by mortgage loan officers and their clients. The *Refinance Analysis* solves this problem. A sample is below. Allow me to walk you through it.

Assumptions

First, I clearly outline the assumptions that will affect the final interest rate. Change the assumptions and the loan terms change (rate and lender credit if any).

Current Loan

This is the first, grey column. This shows the client's current loan type, rate, remaining term (the most important variable), their monthly, annual and remaining life of loan payments.

Best for Cash Flow ← → **Best for Savings**

Across the top of the loan options you will see this row. Below you have the loan options. They are listed in order from which one will provide the best cash flow (lowest payment) for the client to the other extreme: the one that will save them the most money over time (the highest payment). Please note, there simply isn't enough room on the analysis to have an Option 5, 10YF loan, but as the conversation unfolds, if a 10YF loan appears to be a viable option, I simply add it to the analysis. Also, it's important to note, you can cannot really compare fixed rate loans to ARM loans via this analysis as one cannot know the ARM's interest rate once it enters the adjustment phase.

Option 1

I always show the client the loan product they presently have over it's full term. Why? The need for better cashflow is a realistic reason to refinance, plus I know that 99 out of 100 mortgage loan officers are showing the client this option, but not explaining the implications on their true savings—if any. Using the *Refinance Analysis* below, you can see the client's payment will fall $560 per month. An additional $560 per month is likely attractive to nearly any client. However, what clients are not told—but, what the analysis clearly shows—is the majority of this payment change is merely because they extended their loan term by 110 months! They took a loan with 250 remaining payments and spread it back out to 360 months. Of course, their payment will go down. Even at the same interest rate their payment will go down. The good news is the *Refinance Analysis* clearly shows this.

Assumptions:

1st mortgage balance:	$ 334,985
2nd mortgage (HELOC) balance:	$ -
Total mortgage(s) balance:	$ 334,985
Appraised value:	$ 585,000
Loan-to-value ratio (LTV):	57.3%
Combined loan-to-value ratio (CLTV):	57.3%
Program:	N/A
Purpose:	Rate-term refinance
Property type:	Single family
Occupancy:	Owner occupied
Property County, State:	St. Louis, MO
Estimated credit score:	>=740
Escrow:	**Yes**
Open a free ▮▮▮▮▮▮▮▮ *checking:*	**Yes**
Rate lock period:	45 days

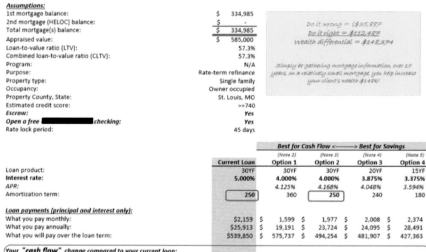

Do it wrong = ($35,887
Do it right = $112,487
Wealth differential = $148,374

Simply be gathering mortgage information over 25 years, on a relatively small mortgage, you help increase your client's wealth $148K!

		Best for Cash Flow <---------> Best for Savings			
		(Note 2)	(Note 3)	(Note 4)	(Note 5)
	Current Loan	Option 1	Option 2	Option 3	Option 4
Loan product:	30YF	30YF	30YF	20YF	15YF
Interest rate:	5.000%	4.000%	4.000%	3.875%	3.375%
APR:		4.125%	4.168%	4.048%	3.594%
Amortization term:	250	360	250	240	180
Loan payments (principal and interest only):					
What you pay monthly:	$2,159	$ 1,599	$ 1,977	$ 2,008	$ 2,374
What you pay annually:	$25,913	$ 19,191	$ 23,724	$ 24,095	$ 28,491
What you will pay over the loan term:	$539,850	$ 575,737	$ 494,254	$ 481,907	$ 427,363
Your "cash flow" change compared to your current loan:					
Your monthly payment change:		$ 560	$ 182	$ 151	$ (215)
Your annual payment change:		$ 6,722	$ 2,189	$ 1,817	$ (2,578)
Your life of loan payment change:		$ (35,887)	$ 45,596	$ 57,943	$ 112,487
Your "savings" change compared to your current loan:					
Your average monthly savings:		$ (100)	$ 182	$ 241	$ 625
Your average annual savings:		$ (1,196)	$ 2,189	$ 2,897	$ 7,499
Your life of loan savings:		$ (35,887)	$ 45,596	$ 57,943	$ 112,487
The estimated cost to refinance:					
Lender related fees:					
Lender origination / processing fee:		$ 995	$ 995	$ 995	$ 995
Lender fee for interest rate chosen:		$ -	$ -	$ -	$ -
Lender credit for interest rate chosen:		$ -	$ -	$ -	$ -
Appraisal fee:		$ 450	$ 450	$ 450	$ 450
Tax service fee:		$ -	$ -	$ -	$ -
Flood letter fee:		$ 16	$ 16	$ 16	$ 16
Credit report fee:		$ 57	$ 57	$ 57	$ 57
▮▮▮ *credit for opening a free* ▮▮▮ *checking:*		$ -	$ -	$ -	$ -
Total "lender related" fees:		$ 1,518	$ 1,518	$ 1,518	$ 1,518
Title company fees:		$ 800	$ 800	$ 800	$ 800
Government fees:		$ 183	$ 183	$ 183	$ 183
Transfer taxes:		$ -	$ -	$ -	$ -
Attorney:		$ -	$ -	$ -	$ -
Fannie Mae 921 form fee (condo's only):		$ -	$ -	$ -	$ -
Second mortgage holder re-subordination fee:		$ -	$ -	$ -	$ -
Total estimated costs:		$ 2,501	$ 2,501	$ 2,501	$ 2,501
"Cash Flow" Breakeven/Payback in months:		4	14	17	-12
"Savings" Breakeven/Payback in months:	NA	-25	14	10	4

Figure 3. Sample Refinance Analysis

Notes

1. Per last appraised value. An appraisal will be required

2. This is a new 30YF loan over 360 months. Your "payment" will fall $560/month and $6,722/year. However, only $182/month of this is due to the lower interest rate. The rest of the "payment" change is simply because you extended your loan term from 250 months back to 360 months. This

45

means you will make 110 additional payments. Once you add these payments you will pay $35,887 MORE over the term of the loan.

3. This is your true "apples-to-apples" comparison. This is a new 30YF loan over 250 months. You will "**save**" $182/month, $2,189/year and $45K over the term of the loan.

4. This is a new 20YF loan over 240 months. Your payment will fall $151/month, $1,817/year, and you will "**save**" $57K over the life of the loan.

5. This is a new 15YF loan over 180 months. Your payment will increase $215/month, $2,578/year, but you will "**save**" $112K over the life of the loan.

Option 2

Next, I always show the client the same loan they have, over the same remaining term, but at the new interest rate. This is their true apples-to-apples savings because you have isolated the payment change based solely on the interest rate. In the comparison below, this is a 30YF loan, but over 250 months. The client's payment will go down—and they will truly save--$182 per month. When you isolate the interest rate variable, the payment change, and true savings are the same.

Option 3

Next I like to show the client the next shorter-term loan product. In this case it is a 20YF loan. The client's loan payment would still do down $151 per month, but while it feels to them like they are saving $151 per month, they are actually saving, on average, $241 per month due to the lower interest rate and shorter term. What a great option. A lower payment plus significant savings.

Option 4

Lastly, I like to show the next shorter-term loan product. In this case it is a 15YF loan. If the client can afford to pay an additional $215 per month, they can refinance to a 15YF loan. To the client it feels like they are paying more per month, and they are, but, on average, they are saving $625 per month due to the lower rate and shorter term. In this case the client's total savings will be $112,487 over 15 years. This is a very good example of why I encourage my wealth manager/CPA referral partners to get a mortgage statement during their annual client meetings and send them to me for analysis. This is a relatively small loan at $334,985, yet working together, we can increase their wealth over 15 years by $112,487—without even touching their assets! I think this is significant.

WAIT! There is one more round of math you need to do. Remember what you learned in The Misguided Focus on Rate? Well, to truly see if it is worth refinancing, we need to do that math on Option 4. I want to know how much of this $112,487 is due to the interest rate and how much is due to the term. So, isolate the term variable, by calculating the payment using a rate of 5% (their current rate).

$334,985, 15YF @ 5% = $2,649/mo x 180 months = **$476,827**

— $334,985, 15YF @ 3.375% = $2,374 x 180 months = **$427,363**

= Savings due to rate: **$49,464**

Hence, it makes sense to refinance. I do this math because sometimes a client can save 95% of the savings without financing. If that is the case, I call that to their attention.

Notes

In this section I re-explain what the spreadsheet calculates to reiterate for those non-spreadsheet-oriented clients.

Caveat: Of course, there is always the option of not paying the additional $215 per month toward one's mortgage and investing it instead. This is a completely viable option and I always defer to the wealth manager / CPA on this. Regardless, the *Refinance Analysis* provides the precise data to the client and their wealth advisor/CPA so they can make a fully educated, intelligent decision without the cloud of a sales pitch.

4.4. Should You Combine 2 (or more) Loans And Refinance?

This is a much trickier question. Again, as you have learned, it's all about the loan term. When you combine two loans, it is extremely unlikely, they will both have the same remaining term. When considering combining two loans (or more) the first thing I do is clearly show the current debt structure and calculate the weighted average interest rate. For example, one of my wealth advisor referral partners in Denver asked me to review a quote and advice from one of the nation's largest lenders. They have won so many awards, personally, I cannot comprehend why with this kind of advice. The clients had a $385k 1st mortgage at 3.875% plus $18k in credit card debt at 15%. The monthly mortgage principal and interest payment was $1879 per month, and the monthly credit card payments were $723 per month. Of course, 15% is a very high rate and it sounds really bad. The other lender suggested they combine both loans into a new 30YF at **4.375%**. Their new monthly payment would be $2,012, or $590 lower than their combined (mortgage plus credit card) payments before. This young couple thought they were saving $590 per month. As noted, first, calculate their weighted average rate:

$385K 30YF mortgage @ 3.875%, 336 remaining payments, monthly principal + interest = **$1,879**

+ $18K credit card debt @ 15%, 30 remaining payments, monthly principal + interest = **$723**

= $403K total debt at a weighted average rate of **3.9%** total monthly principal + interest = **$2,602**

Intuitively you should be thinking, "How can a person's interest rate go up, from 3.9% to 4.375%, yet they are saving money?" You are right to wonder that. They are not saving money. First, yes, 15% is a very high interest rate, but it is on 4.47% of their total debt ($18k / $403k = 4.47%). The reduction in the client's monthly payment was solely because they increased the term on their credit card debt from 30 months to 360 months, and they extended the term on their mortgage from 336 months to 360 months! In fact, if the clients had followed this mortgage company's advice, they would have paid $71k MORE over 30 years! Ultimately, my advice to this young couple was to stay the course. In 30 months, their credit cards will be paid off, and they will have a 30YF mortgage with 306 remaining payments at 3.875%--about .5% below the market rate at that time.

The Combined Refinance Analysis

Below is a sample of my *Combined Refinance Analysis* for the example we just discussed. It follows the same format as the *Refinance Analysis* and again, clearly shows the client and their wealth advisor the precise information they need to make an intelligent, well-educated mortgage decision. It should not be

about selling. It should be about helping.

Assumptions:

1st mortgage balance:	$ 385,000
2nd mortgage (HELOC) balance:	$ 18,000
Total mortgage(s) balance:	$ 403,000
Appraised value:	$ 529,045 (Note 1)
Loan-to-value ratio (LTV):	72.8%
Combined loan-to-value ratio (CLTV):	76.2%
Program:	N/A
Purpose:	Cash-out refinance
Property type:	Single family
Occupancy:	Owner occupied
Property County, State:	Denver, CO
Estimated credit score:	>=760
Escrow:	Yes
Autopay:	N/A

	Current Debt Structure			Potential New Debt Structures			
				(Best for Cash Flow <------------------> Best for Savings)			
	1st Mort	**2nd Mort**	**Total**	**Option 1**	**Option 2**	**Option 3**	**Option 4**
Loan product:	30YF	Credit cards		30YF	30YF	20YF	15YF
Interest rate:	3.875%	15.000%		4.375%	4.375%	4.250%	4.000%
Amortization term:	336	30		360	336	240	180
Loan payments (principal and interest only):							
What you pay monthly:	$1,879	$723	$2,602	$ 2,012	$ 2,082	$ 2,496	$ 2,981
What you pay annually:	$22,553	$8,676	$31,229	$ 24,145	$ 24,988	$ 29,946	$ 35,771
What you will pay over the loan term: (Note 2)	$631,475	$21,690	$653,165	$ 724,363	$ 699,665	$ 598,924	$ 536,570
Your "cash flow" change compared to your current loan:							
Your monthly cash flow change:				$ 590	$ 520	$ 107	$ (379)
Your annual cash flow change:		Cash Flow		$ 7,083	$ 6,241	$ 1,282	$ (4,543)
Your life of loan cash flow change:				$ (71,198)	$ (46,501)	$ 54,241	$ 116,595
Your "savings" change compared to your current loan:							
Your average monthly savings:				$ (198)	$ (138)	$ 226	$ 648
Your average annual savings:		Savings		$ (2,373)	$ (1,661)	$ 2,712	$ 7,773
Your life of loan savings:				$ (71,198)	$ (46,501)	$ 54,241	$ 116,595
The estimated cost to refinance:							
Lender related fees:							
Lender origination / processing fee:				$ 995	$ 995	$ 995	$ 995
Rate discount fee:				$ -	$ -	$ -	$ -
(Lender credit):				$ -	$ -	$ -	$ -
Appraisal fee:				$ 500	$ 500	$ 500	$ 500
Tax service fee:				$ -	$ -	$ -	$ -
Flood letter fee:				$ 16	$ 16	$ 16	$ 16
Credit report fee:				$ 57	$ 57	$ 57	$ 57
Total "lender related" fees:				$ 1,568	$ 1,568	$ 1,568	$ 1,568
Title company fees:				$ 1,300	$ 1,300	$ 1,300	$ 1,300
Government fees:				$ 300	$ 300	$ 300	$ 300
Transfer taxes:				$ -	$ -	$ -	$ -
Fannie Mae 921 form fee (condo's only):				$ -	$ -	$ -	$ -
Second mortgage holder re-subordination fee:				$ -	$ -	$ -	$ -
Total estimated costs:				$ 3,168	$ 3,168	$ 3,168	$ 3,168
Breakeven / Payback (in months, based on your "savings"):				-16	-23	14	5

Chapter 5. Exhibits

1. Comparing Two Loans: *Loan Comparison Worksheet* examples

2. Should You Refinance? *Refinance Analysis* examples

3. Should You Combine Two Loans & Refinance? *Combined Refinance Analysis* examples

Comparing Two Loans: Loan Comparison Worksheet example

Loan Terms:

							Diff
Lender:							
Loan amount:	$	308,000	$	308,000			
Down payment/equity:	$	77,000	$	77,000			
Purchase price/appraised value:	$	385,000	$	385,000	$		-
Product:		30YF		30YF			
Term in months:		360		360			
Rate:		4.250%		4.500%			-0.250%
Payment:	$	1,515	$	1,561	$		(45)
PMI:	$	-	$	-	$		-
Total loan payment:	$	1,515	$	1,561	$		(45)

Variable costs: (Loan Estimate Sections A & B):

Application fee:	$	-	$	-			
Lender fees:	$	-	$	-			
Appraisal:	$	500	$	600			
Credit report:	$	50	$	19			
Application:	$	-	$	395			
Commitment:	$	-	$	385			
Flood report:	$	14	$	8			
Tax service:	$	-	$	80			
Lender credit based on interest rate:	$	-	$	(1,540)			
_____ credit for opening a _____ Checking:	$	-	$	(1,000)			
Total variable costs:	$	564	$	(1,053)	$		1,617

XXX is clearly offering a better rate. They are .25% lower, which equates to you saving $45 per month.

As for costs, we are lower by $1617 at closing.

Breakeven: $1617 / $45 = 36 months.

I think 36 months is a very acceptable breakeven timeframe. Especially as you will likely hold this property for a long time.

So there you go, XXX is better. Proceed forward with them. I will leave your loan open as long as possible in the event something goes awry.

Matt

Comparing Two Loans: Loan Comparison Worksheet example

Loan Terms:

		ABC Bank		XYZ Bank		Diff
Lender:						
Loan amount:	$	645,642	$	645,642		
Down payment/equity:	$	244,358	$	244,358		
Purchase price/appraised value:	$	890,000	$	890,000	$	-
Product:		30YF		30YF		
Term in months:		360		360		
Rate:		4.375%		4.500%		-0.125%
Payment:	$	3,224	$	3,271	$	(48)
PMI:	$	-	$	-	$	-
Total loan payment:	$	**3,224**	$	**3,271**	$	**(48)**

Variable costs: (Loan Estimate Sections A & B):

		ABC Bank		XYZ Bank		Diff
ABC lender fees estimate:	$	1,500	$	-		
VA Funding fee:	$	8,137	$	-		
Appraisal:	$	-	$	400		
Credit report:	$	-	$	32		
Application:	$	-	$	395		
Commitment:	$	-	$	370		
Flood report:	$	-	$	8		
Tax service:	$	-	$	80		
Lender credit based on interest rate:	$	-	$	-		
XYZ Bank credit for opening a _____ Checking:	$	-	$	300		
Total variable costs:	$	**9,637**	$	**1,585**	$	**8,052**

Dear :

I have estimated the ABC Bank numbers, but I think they are close enough to prove my point.

It is not worth paying the $8137 VA funding fee to save .125% in rate. The lower rate will save you $48/month, but the ABC Bank VA loan costs are $8052 higher. The breakeven on that is $8052/$48 = 168 months, or 14 years. That is way too far in the future.

Call me with questions.

Matt

Comparing Two Loans: Loan Comparison Worksheet example

		ABC		XYZ		Diff
Lender:		ABC		XYZ		Diff
Loan amount:	$	360,000	$	360,000		
Down payment/equity:	$	40,000	$	40,000		
Purchase price/appraised value:	$	400,000	$	400,000	$	-
Product:		30YF		30YF		
Term in months:		360		360		
Rate:		5.000%		5.000%		0.000%
Payment:	$	1,933	$	1,933	$	-
PMI:	$	102	$	93	$	9
Total loan payment:	$	2,035	$	2,026	$	9
Variable costs:						
Underwriting fee:	$	340				
Processing fee:	$	250	$	765		
Discount points:	$	-				
Appraisal fee:	$	650	$	400		
Credit report:	$	70	$	32		
Employment verification:	$	40				
Tax service fee:	$	60	$	80		
Flood determination fee:	$	10	$	8		
XYZ Bank free ▮▮▮▮ checking credit:	$	-	$	(900)		
Lender credit for interest chosen:	$	-	*$*	*(900)*		
Total variable costs:	$	1,420	$	(515)	$	1,935

Dear :

This is how I compare two loans--terms & variable fees. As for terms, we have the same rate, but it appears our mortgage insurance is $9 less per month.

When it comes to the variable costs, if you are willing to open a XYZ Bank platinum checking (no fees, $50 minimum balance), XYZ Bank will be $1935 less in closing costs. If you do not want to open the checking account, XYZ Bank will be $1035 less in variable costs at closing.

Again, this comparison as of 10/24. Rates may be different today.

Please call me with any questions.

Sincerely,

Comparing Two Loans: Loan Comparison Worksheet example

Loan Terms:							
Lender:			ABC		XYZ		Diff
Loan amount:	$		424,000	$	424,000		
Down payment/equity:	$		106,000	$	106,000		
Purchase price/appraised value:	$		530,000	$	530,000	$	-
Product:			30YF		30YF		
Term in months:			360		360		
Rate:			4.375%		4.500%		-0.125%
Payment:	$		2,117	$	2,148	$	(31)
PMI:	$		-	$	-	$	-
Total loan payment:	$		**2,117**	$	**2,148**	$	**(31)**

Variable costs: (Loan Estimate Sections A & B):					
ABC Fees:					
Lender fee:	$	995			
Appraisal fee:	$	510			
Credit report fee:	$	59			
	$	1,564			
XYZ Bank Fees:					
Application:			$	395	
Commitment:			$	375	
Appraisal:			$	400	
Tax service:			$	80	
Credit:			$	32	
Flood:			$	9	
Lender credit based on interest rate:			$	(1,590)	
XYZ Bank credit for opening a ▇▇▇ Checking:			$	(1,000)	
Total variable costs:	$	**1,564**	$	**(1,299)**	$	**2,863**

▇▇▇▇▇▇

ABC has a .125% lower rate which eqates to savings to you of $31/month.

On the other hand, our fees are negative $1299, making them $2863 less than ABC.

Breakeven = $2863 / $31 = 92 months or 7.7 years.

So, there you go. I personally think a 7.7 year breakeven is a bit far in the future, but defer to your better judgment about your personal situation.

Sorry for the wrong numbers earlier. Monday mornings are busy and I was working too fast.

Any questions, call me.

Matt

Should You Refinance? Refinance Analysis example

Assumptions:

1st mortgage balance:	$ 822,967	
2nd mortgage (HELOC) balance:	$ -	
Total mortgage(s) balance:	$ 822,967	
Appraised value:	$ 2,300,000	(Note 1)
Loan-to-value ratio (LTV):	35.8%	
Combined loan-to-value ratio (CLTV):	35.8%	
Program:	N/A	
Purpose:	Rate-term refinance	
Property type:	Single family	
Occupancy:	Owner occupied	
Property County, State:	Wichita, KS	
Estimated credit score:	>=740	
Escrow:	No	
Open a free ▮▮▮▮ checking:	Yes	
Rate lock period:	45 days	

		Best for Cash Flow <--------> Best for Savings			
		(Note 2)	(Note 3)	(Note 4)	(Note 5)
	Current Loan	Option 1	Option 2	Option 3	Option 4
Loan product:	30YF	30YF	30YF	20YF	15YF
Interest rate:	5.500%	4.375%	4.375%	4.125%	3.990%
APR:		4.375%	4.375%	4.125%	3.990%
Amortization term:	255	360	255	240	180
Loan payments (principal and interest only):					
What you pay monthly:	$5,479	$ 4,109	$ 4,962	$ 5,041	$ 6,083
What you pay annually:	$65,750	$ 49,307	$ 59,546	$ 60,497	$ 72,999
What you will pay over the loan term:	$1,397,186	$ 1,479,223	$ 1,265,353	$ 1,209,934	$ 1,094,988
Your "cash flow" change compared to your current loan:					
Your monthly payment change:	Payment Change	$ 1,370	$ 517	$ 438	$ (604)
Your annual payment change:		$ 16,443	$ 6,204	$ 5,253	$ (7,249)
Your life of loan payment change:		$ (82,037)	$ 131,834	$ 187,253	$ 302,199
Your "savings" change compared to your current loan:					
Your average monthly savings:	True Savings Change	$ (228)	$ 517	$ 780	$ 1,679
Your average annual savings:		$ (2,735)	$ 6,204	$ 9,363	$ 20,147
Your life of loan savings:		$ (82,037)	$ 131,834	$ 187,253	$ 302,199
The estimated cost to refinance:					
Lender related fees:					
Lender origination / processing fee:		$ 770	$ 770	$ 770	770
Lender fee for interest rate chosen:		$ -	$ -	$ -	-
Lender credit for interest rate chosen:		$ (2,848)	$ (2,848)	$ (2,848)	(2,848)
Appraisal fee:		$ 400	$ 400	$ 400	400
Tax service fee:		$ 80	$ 80	$ 80	80
Flood letter fee:		$ 8	$ 8	$ 8	8
Credit report fee:		$ 32	$ 32	$ 32	32
XYZ Bank credit for opening a free ▮▮▮▮ checking:		$ (1,000)	$ (1,000)	$ (1,000)	(1,000)
Total "lender related" fees:		$ (2,558)	$ (2,558)	$ (2,558)	(2,558)
Title company fees:		$ 1,535	$ 1,535	$ 1,535	1,535
Government fees:		$ 200	$ 200	$ 200	200
Transfer taxes:		$ 823	$ 823	$ 823	823
Attorney:		$ -	$ -	$ -	-
Fannie Mae 921 form fee (condo's only):		$ -	$ -	$ -	-
Second mortgage holder re-subordination fee:		$ -	$ -	$ -	-
Total estimated costs:		$ -	$ -	$ -	-

Should You Refinance? Refinance Analysis example

Assumptions:

1st mortgage balance:	$ 963,550
2nd mortgage (HELOC) balance:	$ -
Total mortgage(s) balance:	$ 963,550
Appraised value:	$ 1,500,000 (Note 1)
Loan-to-value ratio (LTV):	64.2%
Combined loan-to-value ratio (CLTV):	64.2%
Program:	N/A
Purpose:	Rate-term refinance
Property type:	Single family
Occupancy:	Owner occupied
Property County, State:	St. Louis, MO
Estimated credit score:	>=740
Escrow:	Yes
Open a free ▮▮▮▮ checking:	Yes
Rate lock period:	45 days

		Best for Cash Flow <---------> Best for Savings			
		(Note 2)	(Note 3)	(Note 4)	(Note 5)
	Current Loan	Option 1	Option 2	Option 3	Option 4
Loan product:	30YF	30YF	30YF	20YF	15YF
Interest rate:	5.000%	4.250%	4.250%	3.750%	3.625%
APR:		4.234%	4.229%	3.728%	3.597%
Amortization term:	265	360	265	240	180
Loan payments (principal and interest only):					
What you pay monthly:	$6,012	$ 4,740	$ 5,611	$ 5,713	$ 6,948
What you pay annually:	$72,149	$ 56,881	$ 67,336	$ 68,553	$ 83,371
What you will pay over the loan term:	$1,593,287	$ 1,706,431	$ 1,487,014	$ 1,371,066	$ 1,250,559
Your "cash flow" change compared to your current loan:					
Your monthly payment change:		$ 1,272	$ 401	$ 300	$ (935)
Your annual payment change:		$ 15,268	$ 4,812	$ 3,596	$ (11,222)
Your life of loan payment change:		$ (113,145)	$ 106,273	$ 222,220	$ 342,728
Your "savings" change compared to your current loan:					
Your average monthly savings:		$ (314)	$ 401	$ 926	$ 1,904
Your average annual savings:		$ (3,771)	$ 4,812	$ 11,111	$ 22,849
Your life of loan savings:		$ (113,145)	$ 106,273	$ 222,220	$ 342,728
The estimated cost to refinance:					
Lender related fees:					
Lender origination / processing fee:		$ 770	$ 995	$ 995	$ 995
Lender fee for interest rate chosen:		$ -	$ -	$ -	$ -
Lender credit for interest rate chosen:		$ (2,408)	$ (2,408)	$ -	$ (2,408)
Appraisal fee:		$ 400	$ 500	$ 500	$ 500
Tax service fee:		$ 80	$ -	$ -	$ -
Flood letter fee:		$ 8	$ 16	$ 16	$ 16
Credit report fee:		$ 32	$ 57	$ 57	$ 57
XYZ Bank credit for opening a free ▮▮ checking:		$ (1,000)	$ (1,000)	$ (1,000)	$ (1,000)
Total "lender related" fees:		$ (2,118)	$ (1,840)	$ 568	$ (1,840)
Title company fees:		$ 1,000	$ 1,000	$ 1,000	$ 1,000
Government fees:		$ 183	$ 183	$ 183	$ 183
Transfer taxes:		$ -	$ -	$ -	$ -
Attorney:		$ -	$ -	$ -	$ -
Fannie Mae 921 form fee (condo's only):		$ -	$ -	$ -	$ -
Second mortgage holder re-subordination fee:		$ -	$ -	$ -	$ -
Total estimated costs:		$ (935)	$ (657)	$ 1,751	$ (657)

Should You Refinance? Refinance Analysis example

Assumptions:

1st mortgage balance:	$ 137,797
2nd mortgage (HELOC) balance:	$ -
Total mortgage(s) balance:	$ 137,797
Appraised value:	$ 359,000 *(Note 1)*
Loan-to-value ratio (LTV):	38.4%
Combined loan-to-value ratio (CLTV):	38.4%
Program:	N/A
Purpose:	Rate-term refinance
Property type:	Single family
Occupancy:	Owner occupied
Property County, State:	St. Louis, MO
Estimated credit score:	>=740
You will establish a free ██████ checking:	Yes
Rate lock period:	45 days

		Best for Cash Flow <---------> Best for Savings			
	Current Loan	Option 1 *(Note 2)*	Option 2 *(Note 3)*	Option 3 *(Note 4)*	Option 4 *(Note 5)*
Loan product:	TBD	15YF	15YF	10YF	
Interest rate:	5.875%	4.750%	4.750%	4.000%	
APR:		5.189%	5.206%	4.620%	
Amortization term:	172	180	172	120	
Loan payments (principal and interest only):					
What you pay monthly:	$1,186	$ 1,072	$ 1,105	$ 1,395	
What you pay annually:	$14,235	$ 12,862	$ 13,262	$ 16,742	
What you will pay over the loan term:	$204,267	$ 192,929	$ 190,317	$ 167,415	
Your "cash flow" change compared to your current loan:					
Your monthly payment change:		$ 114	$ 81	$ (209)	
Your annual payment change:		$ 1,373	$ 972	$ (2,507)	
Your life of loan payment change:		$ 11,338	$ 13,951	$ 36,852	
Your "savings" change compared to your current loan:					
Your average monthly savings:		$ 63	$ 81	$ 307	
Your average annual savings:		$ 756	$ 972	$ 3,685	
Your life of loan savings:		$ 11,338	$ 13,951	$ 36,852	
The estimated cost to refinance:					
Lender related fees:					
Application:		$ 395	$ 395	$ 395	
Commitment:		$ 370	$ 370	$ 370	
Appraisal:		$ 400	$ 400	$ 400	
Credit report:		$ 32	$ 32	$ 32	
Tax service:		$ 80	$ 80	$ 80	
Flood:		$ 8	$ 8	$ 8	
Lender charge for interest rate chosen:		$ -	$ -	$ -	
Lender credit for interest rate chosen:		$ -	$ -	$ (688)	
Credit for opening a free ABC Bank ██ checking:		$ (300)	$ (300)	$ (300)	
Total "lender related" fees:		$ 985	$ 985	$ 297	
Title company fees:		$ 800	$ 800	$ 800	
Government fees:		$ 180	$ 180	$ 180	
Transfer taxes:		$ -	$ -	$ -	
Attorney:		$ -	$ -	$ -	
Fannie Mae 921 form fee (condo's only):		$ -	$ -	$ -	
Second mortgage holder re-subordination fee:		$ -	$ -	$ -	
Total estimated costs:		$ 1,965	$ 1,965	$ 1,277	
"Cash Flow" Breakeven/Payback in months:		17	24	-6	
"Savings" Breakeven/Payback in months:		24	24	4	

Should You Refinance? Refinance Analysis example

Assumptions:

1st mortgage balance:	$ 963,550
2nd mortgage (HELOC) balance:	$ -
Total mortgage(s) balance:	$ 963,550
Appraised value:	$ 1,500,000 (Note 1)
Loan-to-value ratio (LTV):	64.2%
Combined loan-to-value ratio (CLTV):	64.2%
Program:	N/A
Purpose:	Rate-term refinance
Property type:	Single family
Occupancy:	Owner occupied
Property County, State:	St. Louis, MO
Estimated credit score:	>=740
Escrow:	Yes
Open a free ▓▓▓▓▓ checking:	Yes
Rate lock period:	45 days

		Best for Cash Flow <-------> Best for Savings			
		(Note 2)	(Note 3)	(Note 4)	(Note 5)
	Current Loan	Option 1	Option 2	Option 3	Option 4
Loan product:	30YF	30YF	30YF	20YF	15YF
Interest rate:	5.000%	4.250%	4.250%	3.750%	3.625%
APR:		4.234%	4.229%	3.728%	3.597%
Amortization term:	265	360	265	240	180
Loan payments (principal and interest only):					
What you pay monthly:	$6,012	$ 4,740	$ 5,611	$ 5,713	$ 6,948
What you pay annually:	$72,149	$ 56,881	$ 67,336	$ 68,553	$ 83,371
What you will pay over the loan term:	$1,593,287	$ 1,706,431	$ 1,487,014	$ 1,371,066	$ 1,250,559
Your "cash flow" change compared to your current loan:					
Your monthly payment change:		$ 1,272	$ 401	$ 300	$ (935)
Your annual payment change:		$ 15,268	$ 4,812	$ 3,596	$ (11,222)
Your life of loan payment change:		$ (113,145)	$ 106,273	$ 222,220	$ 342,728
Your "savings" change compared to your current loan:					
Your average monthly savings:		$ (314)	$ 401	$ 926	$ 1,904
Your average annual savings:		$ (3,771)	$ 4,812	$ 11,111	$ 22,849
Your life of loan savings:		$ (113,145)	$ 106,273	$ 222,220	$ 342,728
The estimated cost to refinance:					
Lender related fees:					
Lender origination / processing fee:		$ 770	$ 995	$ 995	$ 995
Lender fee for interest rate chosen:		$ -	$ -	$ -	$ -
Lender credit for interest rate chosen:		$ (2,408)	$ (2,408)	$ -	$ (2,408)
Appraisal fee:		$ 400	$ 500	$ 500	$ 500
Tax service fee:		$ 80	$ -	$ -	$ -
Flood letter fee:		$ 8	$ 16	$ 16	$ 16
Credit report fee:		$ 32	$ 57	$ 57	$ 57
XYZ Bank credit for opening a free ▓▓ checking:		$ (1,000)	$ (1,000)	$ (1,000)	$ (1,000)
Total "lender related" fees:		$ (2,118)	$ (1,840)	$ 568	$ (1,840)
Title company fees:		$ 1,000	$ 1,000	$ 1,000	$ 1,000
Government fees:		$ 183	$ 183	$ 183	$ 183
Transfer taxes:		$ -	$ -	$ -	$ -
Attorney:		$ -	$ -	$ -	$ -
Fannie Mae 921 form fee (condo's only):		$ -	$ -	$ -	$ -
Second mortgage holder re-subordination fee:		$ -	$ -	$ -	$ -
Total estimated costs:		$ (935)	$ (657)	$ 1,751	$ (657)

This borrower was concerned that their second mortgage rate was so high. However, their weighted average rate was only 4.279%--lower than every option available in the market. I showed them the impact of combining both loans into one. It was a bad outcome. I convinced them to simply pay as much as possible monthly toward their second mortgage.

Assumptions:

1st mortgage balance:	$ 570,342
2nd mortgage (HELOC) balance:	$ 75,300
Total mortgage(s) balance:	$ 645,642
Appraised value:	$ 890,000 *(Note 1)*
Loan-to-value ratio (LTV):	64.1%
Combined loan-to-value ratio (CLTV):	72.5%
Program:	N/A
Purpose:	Cash-out refinance
Property type:	Single family
Occupancy:	Owner occupied
Property County, State:	Denver, CO
Estimated credit score:	>=760
Escrow:	Yes
Autopay:	N/A

	Current Debt Structure			Potential New Debt Structures			
				(Best for Cash Flow <------------> Best for Savings)			
	1st Mort	2nd Mort	Total	Option 1	Option 2	Option 3	Option 4
Loan product:	30YF	HELOC		30YF	30YF	20YF	15YF
Interest rate:	3.875%	7.240%		4.500%	4.500%	4.250%	4.125%
Amortization term:	325	325		360	325	240	180
Loan payments (principal and interest only):							
What you pay monthly:	$2,837	$456	$3,293 $	3,271 $	3,440 $	3,998 $	4,816
What you pay annually:	$34,038	$5,472	$39,510 $	39,256 $	41,286 $	47,976 $	57,795
What you will pay over the loan term: *(Note 2)*	$921,875	$223,500	$1,145,375 $	1,177,694 $	1,118,157 $	959,529 $	866,930
Your "cash flow" change compared to your current loan:							
Your monthly cash flow change:			$	21 $	(148) $	(705) $	(1,524)
Your annual cash flow change:	Payment Change		$	254 $	(1,775) $	(8,466) $	(18,285)
Your life of loan cash flow change:			$	(32,319) $	27,218 $	185,846 $	278,445
Your "savings" change compared to your current loan:							
Your average monthly savings:			$	(90) $	84 $	774 $	1,547
Your average annual savings:	Savings Change		$	(1,077) $	1,005 $	9,292 $	18,563
Your life of loan savings:			$	(32,319) $	27,218 $	185,846 $	278,445
The estimated cost to refinance:							
Lender related fees:							
Application:			$	395 $	395 $	395 $	395
Commitment:			$	370 $	370 $	370 $	370
Appraisal:			$	400 $	400 $	400 $	400
Credit report:			$	32 $	32 $	32 $	32
Flood:			$	8 $	8 $	8 $	8
Tax service:			$	80 $	80 $	80 $	80
Rate discount:			$	- $	- $	- $	-
Lender credit for interest rate:			$	- $	- $	- $	-
XYZ Bank credit for opening a ▮▮▮ checking account:			$	(300) $	(300) $	(300) $	(300)
Total "lender related" fees:			$	985 $	985 $	985 $	985
Title company fees:			$	1,300 $	1,300 $	1,300 $	1,300
Government fees:			$	300 $	300 $	300 $	300
Transfer taxes:			$	- $	- $	- $	-
Fannie Mae 921 form fee (condo's only):			$	- $	- $	- $	-
Second mortgage holder re-subordination fee:			$	- $	- $	- $	-
Total estimated costs:			$	2,585 $	2,585 $	2,585 $	2,585
Breakeven / Payback (in months, based on your "savings"):				-29	31	3	2

Figure 4. Should You Combine Two Loans & Refinance? Combined Refinance Analysis example

About The Author

Matt Gallagher loves to educate borrowers, centers of influence and to **save people money**. Really save them money, not just lower their loan payment(s). This passion has earned him the distinction of being one of the highest producing mortgage bankers in the Midwest. Matt started his career 30 years ago in Commercial Lending with one of the region's most entrepreneurial banks, and then spent several years in institutional equity trading. His diverse financial and business background served as the foundation for his creation of his Fiduciary Mortgage Lending practice, which he has grown over the past 13 years through partnerships with leading financial firms.

Matt is renowned for his ability to consult individual clients on their mortgage financing needs and provide quantitative and clear analysis that not only helps the client select the right mortgage program for their needs but assists the referral partner in managing this important debt product as part of the client's overall wealth plan. Fiduciary Mortgage Lending has made Matt more than just another mortgage professional making a loan for a client, he is a valued consulting partner for hundreds of Registered Investment Advisors (RIA's) & CPAs nationwide. Clients and Advisors alike turn to Matt for his professional, non-biased approach that puts the client's interests first, and makes the process work for their needs.

Matt is a Mortgage Loan Officer for A Direct Lender in Saint Louis, MO, and in this role can offer unique, customizable mortgage solutions for clients throughout the United States.

Matt earned his B.S. degree at Westminster College and his MBA from St. Louis University. When not in the office, Matt and his wife Tyra are the proud parents of two college-aged sons: Harry & Sam, and a patience-testing border collie puppy, Astro.

You can contact Matt at fiduciarymortgagelending@outlook.com